The Journey

The Journey

Les Blacklock

Illustrated by Rick Allen

BLACKLOCK NATURE PHOTOGRAPHY

Introduction

by Fran Blacklock

Les loved nothing better than to take friends with him on a hike through our woods. They would see things they probably would never have noticed if Les hadn't stopped to point out something like the pellets at the foot of a hollow tree where porcupines had a den, or the flowers of wild ginger, hidden under its leaves. A favorite in winter was to find wing prints on the snow left by a ruffed grouse as it flew up from its resting place under the snow. A special treat would be to come upon a snowshoe hare in its white winter coat holding still in its *form*. In this book you will have a chance to join Les on a walk through our woods, sharing in his ever-present sense of wonder.

When our story begins, Les was on his way to keep the wood stove going at our son and daughter-in-law's house next door. As always, he was watching for signs of wildlife whether in the trees or on the ground. What he found was something in the snow that puzzled him. He hurried back home, rushed over to our bookcase and grabbed Olaus Murie's *A Field Guide to Animal Tracks*. Comparing the picture in the book with what he saw in the snow, he knew for sure what had made the tracks.

I didn't see Les again until he came home at dusk. Even then he didn't stop for more than a bite of dinner before going upstairs to write down with a pencil his experiences of that day exactly as you will read about them. For two more days he continued where he had stopped the day before and wrote about it at the end of each day.

Les planned that this story would become part of his next book, *Listen to the Land*. It would contain stories showing how people and wildlife could share this planet in harmony. However, Parkinson's Disease gradually took away Les' ability to photograph and write, and *Listen to the Land* was never finished.

After Les died August 30, 1995, I knew that somehow *The Journey* should be published so that more people could enjoy it. After puzzling how that could happen, I called my friend and nearby neighbor, author Carol Bly. She invited me to come over, and after a friendly visit, I left a typed manuscript on her dining room table, and asked, if she had time, would she read it and give me any suggestions she had on how to best use Les' story?

Almost the next day I got a letter from Carol. "<u>Wonderful.</u> I see it as a little book that would just plain give people immense happiness, as it did me." I have taken Carol's advice.

Rick Allen traversed the same route Les took, and made the illustrations to accompany Les' words.

You are now invited to
come with Les on his adventure.

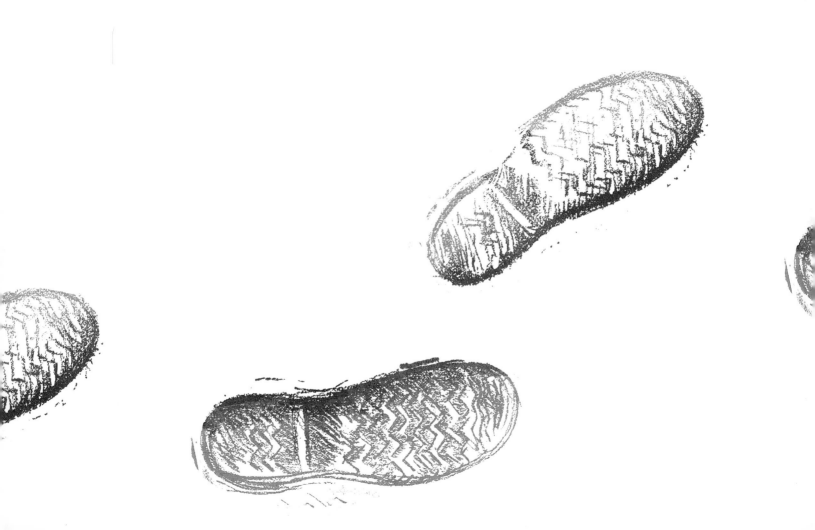

Day One

It is early January. Son Craig and daughter-in-law Nadine are in Minneapolis this week on business, so several times each day I walk the woods path to their house to feed their antique Round Oak wood stove.

An inch of fresh snow, on top of a meager three-inch base, is cohesive enough to mold the zig-zag prints of my Sorrel boots sharp and clean. My eyes habitually search for and try to identify the many wildlife tracks, mostly gray squirrel.

Today there was a stopper. A walking something had crossed the trail and headed inland, away from our little lake. This track was new to me. The animal dragged its feet between steps, and placed its hind footprints on top of the front ones. The track looked like a tiny, two-and-a-half-inch-wide sled had passed by, with hand-like prints in the sled tracks every five inches.

The animal had its toes together when it stepped down through the surface of the snow, then spread them on the harder crust beneath, so the spread prints were partly hidden. This made track-book identification difficult, but the mystery of it intriguing.

Gray squirrels sometimes walk a few steps, but if they're going more than a few feet, they hop, in their familiar arching bounds. This creature walked and walked.

I followed the tracks which led between my wood piles, across our driveway circle, down into and up out of Talking Creek ravine, then straight east, away from the lake, with no sign of change of mind.

Early winter dark was coming on, so I stopped tracking for the night.

Day Two

The weather held a few degrees below freezing, so the tracks maintained their clarity. I studied the prints with A Field Guide to Animal Tracks in hand. The foot-dragging was an exception for an animal this size, and there were very few tail marks. But I found enough clear evidence to positively identify the traveler. It had to be a muskrat, a rather small one.

But why was this water animal out hiking cross-country in mid-winter, when his fellow muskrats were cozy in their bank burrows or cattail-sedge-moss lodges?

I remembered reading somewhere that muskrat mating could start now, but I would think that would be more apt to happen in Missouri than in Minnesota, where minus 50 degrees F. is possible this time of year.

And yet here we are in an unusual warm spell, with days near thawing and nights in the teens. Even so, how did he know this warm weather would hold? Was this muskrat a weather forecaster?

I ate a substantial, early lunch and started tracking. The steady walking gait continued east and southeast, varying only to pick the least cluttered route.

I had to bend my trail more than he did his, because he could walk through alder thickets and under impenetrable windfalls that I avoided. He seemed not to care a whit what sort of habitat lay ahead. We started with easy going among the trunks of northern hardwoods, then crossed an alder moat and a black spruce-tamarack bog. You'd swear he knew the route and had been there before. His tracks showed no hesitancy. Was he going a certain compass direction, or was there an ever-so-faint perfume saying, "here I am, come find me!"?

The muskrat and I were not alone. Soon after we left our woods-road driveway his tracks were crossing more signs of other species, especially under the balsams and in the alder swamps. The stitchery tracks of a ruffed grouse wound a curving pattern like a sewing machine gone wild. Red squirrels' smaller prints replaced the grays' and there were tracks of mink, weasels, red fox, snowshoe hare, shrews, voles, white-footed mice, three trotting coyotes, and the pigeon-toed tracks of a porcupine.

Because the drag marks made the sled-runner
tracks of the muskrat so easy to follow, there was no
danger of my losing him in the maze. I quietly thanked him
for taking me into this wildlife center. And center it was!
Where the tracks were the thickest, the many jaws
flattened the snow to floor-like smoothness
around the

broad trunk of a giant sugar maple, obviously the den tree of the porcupine. A cave-like entrance at ground level was piled to overflowing with porcupine droppings from inside the tree. High up in the crown I could see the pale gold branches where Porky had chewed off the bark. The tree was not only his home, but a food source, too.

I crossed the snow-pack and picked up the muskrat's trail on the far side. This was easy tracking. Wherever I lost the trail in a grass or shrub thicket, I'd just cross his line of travel on the far side and pick it up again.

I couldn't help but think that this small animal,
weighing perhaps two pounds, was in great danger that
far from water, and most wet areas are sealed over by
ice now. He cannot run fast or climb trees to escape
predators, so a chance meeting with one of those
coyotes, a fox or a mink would probably be fatal.

But on he went, steadily striding through the forest.
It took a rather major barrier to cause him to back up
and detour. Only three or four times did he change his
game plan. Even then there was no wasted time, no
seeming frustration. Like a practiced maze-solver, he
just walked back a few steps and tried a
different route.

He lost only a
few seconds
and was
again on his way.

He seemed so sure of himself it was hard to believe he had never been there before, but certainly he had not. He had moved from his birthplace when forcefully evicted by his mother last fall, but very likely followed a water route to his chosen wintering spot. So this over-land expedition was a brand-new experience for him, very different from the cattail-sedge-waterlilly-willow-alder habitat he had known since his birth last spring.

Beyond the bog a rolling hardwood forest made easy going for both of us. Suddenly he veered sharp right and

climbed straight up the steepest hill around. I could see open sky beyond the crest, and guessed that we were approaching a neighbor's hay field.

A second spruce-tamarack bog was easy to cross—for him. Snowshoe hare trails between the sphagnum-and-shrub hummocks were smooth and relatively straight, kept that way by dozens of generations of hares. But at my level, rough spruce branches brushed off my wool cap several times, and forced me to push through where my leader walked unimpeded.

I was right. The muskrat and I came out of the forest onto the first of several large, undulating fields. The borders of the fields were all gracefully curved, following forest edges and the rounds of bottom wetlands. I could see the county road on the far side of the field. Hay stubble stuck up through this winter's very shallow snow. I was impressed by the beauty of the landscape which I had not seen from that hill before. But I doubt the muskrat cared about scenic beauty. He had never seen any hayfield before, but instead of contemplating his new surroundings, he turned east again along the edge of the field, staying in the short stubble, but hugging close against the tall grass. The snow had melted to the ground in many places along this sheltered forest edge, but as long as I followed the field edge, I found his tracks in the scattered snow patches. He was taking a long but easy route, staying near the cover of the forest. He did cut across a narrow bay of the field, indicating some feeling of urgency. The long five-inch steps also said that he was earnestly pressing on (the track book shows three inches between steps of a walking muskrat).

We followed the edge of the first field around south toward the county road. Without hesitation he climbed straight up the steep road bank. But the blacktop road itself stopped him. He immediately turned east and walked along the outer edge of the mowed grass along the road, just as he had on the edge of the field. Only this time he would be within a few feet of passing cars, if any came along this little-used road.

An opening in the tall grass on the bank looked like a possible passage down the slope to the next hayfield. He started down. It dead ended in a thick mass of

waist-high grass and weeds. Here was one of the few
places he backtracked. But several rods farther east he
did find a way down. It was getting late, so I marked the
spot, hiked the two miles home via the county road and
our half-mile driveway, got out my maps and references,
and wrote these
words.

Day Three

    Today I had to know. Where did he come from? How did he get above the ice that covers our little lake? Is there open water down by the beaver dam? So I backtracked.

    Amazingly, on this third day, the tracks were still detail-clear. It's about two hundred feet from our houses through the hardwoods down the slope to water level, another two hundred feet through a sedge-pocked maze of pools and passages to the seven-acre pond we call Moosetail Lake.

The last thirty feet or so is a lake-circling necklace of islands composed mainly of thigh-deep carpets of leatherleaf, with scattered alders, a few tamaracks, willows, sweetgale, cattails, and a number of other plants usually found in northern bogs. The base of these islands is sphagnum moss, and this floating rim goes up and down with the water level depending on precipitation and what the beavers do with their dam, down at the far end of the pond.

I backtracked the muskrat to one of these leather-leaf islands, about thirty by forty feet, an almost ogague thicket, still holding all of its dark maroon leaves. He had ventured out a few feet from the island in several directions, but had always circled back, like drawing flower petals in the snow.

Some of his tracks on the snow-covered ice seemed to come from nowhere until I traced them to a hole in a small thicket of sedge. But when I removed a chopper mitt and reached a bare hand down into the hole, I hit ice, not water. Obviously it had been open when the tracks were made, but not now, and the trail I had been following didn't start from there.

At one place he had ventured out about thirty feet onto the lake ice as if he were going to cross to the other shore, then thought better of it and came back to the thick cover. Wouldn't an eagle or a goshawk have liked to have seen him in mid-lake?

I circled the island outside of all the tracks except those of his big journey, and decided there had to be a connection between above and below the ice there. I was aware of a muskrat house near our canoe landing, but the only entrances to that were under the ice. So I peered into the thigh-high thicket from all sides.

There was a dark <u>something</u> in there, toward the opposite side, directly under the tallest shrubs on the island. I circled around and pressed in. There it was; a low pile of brown, shredded, partially-decomposed vegetation, typical muskrat building material. Three thick stems of speckled alder stuck up through the frozen mass, and were taller than I can reach. About two dozen smaller alder stems surrounded the structure. Five bright red stems of roundleaf dogwood further pointed out that <u>here</u> was the site. Once you <u>know</u> all of this, it's easy to find it next time by. But without the tracks I'd never have noticed it.

The mass, only twenty-four by twenty-eight inches, and a foot high, was far too small for a muskrat house, which can be eight or more feet in diameter and three feet or so above the water line. I got down on my knees to study the pile, and there was the connection to the under-ice world. A round hole at the very top of the heap was plugged by a round ball of the same brown stem-root-moss stuff as the rest. Expecting it to be frozen stiff, I reached down and easily lifted the ball from the hole. Soft and spongy, it was quite dry and obviously good insulation. Another ball was deeper in the tube, and there may have been more. I replaced the ball, which reminded me of a softball that had been batted so many times that the hide came off and it wasn't quite round any more.

Around the perimeter of the island were little lunch places, bits of sedge stems nipped off in neat little curves by sharp muskrat teeth. The broad tops of the sedge leaves were tan and lifeless, but the sharply triangular stems were summer green just above the ice. Perhaps these green stems were the reason for the feeding station. Are the sedge stems more tasty above the ice than below? Did he come up for fresh air and basking in the sun as well as for the green sedge stems?

Except for the few short loops of tracks off the island, the muskrat's activities were well hidden. If he stayed in the thick cover of the leatherleaf as he quietly snacked and sunbathed, he could have come here often without detection by predators. Perhaps he did.

I don't know if there was a small chamber in the pile for lunching or resting above the ice or not. The whole structure was so small that I think its sole purpose was insulation to keep the hole through the ice from freezing. It is only about two hundred feet from there to the muskrat's house, with a warm room for napping and feeding.

Some questions remain unanswered. Did the muskrat know when he came up through the hole in the ice and pushed the door-balls aside that he was going on his journey? Did he know when he so carefully placed the insulating doors back in place that he would probably never be back? Did he know when he ate the meal of sedge stems that he needed that food for energy for the long hike? Did he know that all ahead of time or was it a faint whiff of scent or a solar clock saying "it's time" that sent him on his way?

Or was it the unusually warm winter day, near the thaw mark, the promise of spring?

Day Three Continued — More Tracking

Cloudy. Snow forecast. I knew where the muskrat came from. Now, where was he going?

I drove out to the county road and east to where I had left the trail, parked the car and again picked up the tracks where they dropped down the highway bank toward the second field. At the base of the bank, the muskrat got into a tight thicket of grass and sedge, a small pocket wetland. I didn't even try to track him there. I pushed through the thicket and came out onto the second field almost the same place he did.

And there we went again, following the curved edge of the mowed grass, far back from the road—the same pattern as yesterday, but around a different field. Up and down we went, in pleasing sweeps along bordering hardwoods, mixed conifer-hardwood forests and spruce bogs.

Way at the back end of the field, behind the rolling hills, I felt the wildness of remote fields that are often visited by wildlife. No one is back there all year except during haying and perhaps a hunter or two after deer or grouse. I want to go back in other seasons, at dawn and at dusk, very quietly and very slowly stalking that edge, stopping for long looks, perhaps sitting with knees up to steady my binoculars. There would be many possibilities. Deer, of course, and fox, skunk, woodchuck, coyote, possibly a bear. In migration, many kinds of birds.

The scene ahead stopped my daydreaming. There came the three coyote tracks, up out of a bog, walking toward the field. They would, of course, intercept the path of my little muskrat.

And there ahead, where they met, was the sign of a skirmish. Tall grass was beaten down, matted flat at the edge of the stubble.

It was almost too much to ask that a small water animal, slow moving, almost black against the white snow, could walk overland for several miles without being detected.

Being a naturalist, I should accept any outcome as okay. That's the way nature is. Coyotes have to eat, too. And yet, because we'd traveled together, and the little guy was from our own lake, I had sorta hoped...

Hey! There were his tracks, in snow patches beyond the messed up grass. And there went the coyote tracks, onto the field and over the hill.

The muskrat's steps were as deliberate as before, his five-inch pace uninterrupted. He had come through ahead of the coyotes, and apparently his scent had for some reason caused the middle coyote (they were traveling abreast) to roll and scratch the ground at that point. Why they didn't follow the muskrat tracks, I'll never know.

So on we went, curving with the field edge until, on the way to the county road, we followed the edge of a sedge marsh, several acres in size. Was _this_ his destination? I couldn't see a single muskrat house in the whole marsh, but...

Where our trail got closest to the marsh, he turned and started straight across it. I followed, but not far. The ice was at two levels. The top level had frozen, the water had dropped several inches, then the bottom level had frozen. The top layer wouldn't quite hold my weight. Step, CRASH! Step, CRASH! Get outa here!

Once more I worked the edge. Maybe I could pick up his trail on the other side. The marsh went all the way back to the county road, and so did I. As I started to follow the bottom edge of the steep road bank, I came to a small frozen pond of open ice. Here, too, it was in two layers, and from between the two layers of ice came his tracks. He then hiked straight up the road bank.

This time there was no hesitation. As soon as he got up to the blacktop he crossed the road and walked between the only two houses anywhere around. As he was crossing the far ditch, he jumped twice, the only variation from his determined walk since leaving our lake. A car must have come by at that time. I would have jumped, too, if I had never seen a car before and then have one zoom by twenty feet away at fifty-five miles per hour!

Rather than stir up a misunderstanding by snooping through someone's yard in broad daylight, I pushed the door bell of the nearest house. This is how I met our neighbors (two miles away), Bill and Karen Ackerson. I told Bill my mission and he invited me up into their living room. He led me to sliding glass doors that open onto a deck, and indicated their dog's house at the far edge of the lawn. Two days earlier, he told me, the dog was excited about seeing something through the glass doors. Bill went up to the glass to honor the dog's barking, and there was a muskrat walking past the dog house!

It was, of course, my muskrat. And here was proof that the little guy had come all that way the first day from our lake, by 1:30 P.M. What are the odds against two people having very different experiences with the same wild muskrat the same day, two miles apart, and then meeting and sharing those experiences?

It started to snow, so I excused myself and resumed tracking, through a hardwood forest. The snow was getting thicker fast, but even so, that track was so distinctive that I could follow it until it was completely obliterated. That is, until the muskrat entered waist-high grass along the edge of a spruce bog. I half-circled the bog, but the heavy snow soon covered all tracks and I lost him.

But I'm not going to fret over the little guy, and I'll tell you why. He had already rambled over two-and-a-half miles when I lost him, and he had reached that point early afternoon two days before, the same day he left our little lake. He'd had two relatively warm winter days since then to find a female (or two) who would accept him, and to find or build some sort of shelter.

I've just checked the Geological Survey maps of our area (the ones with the contour lines, green

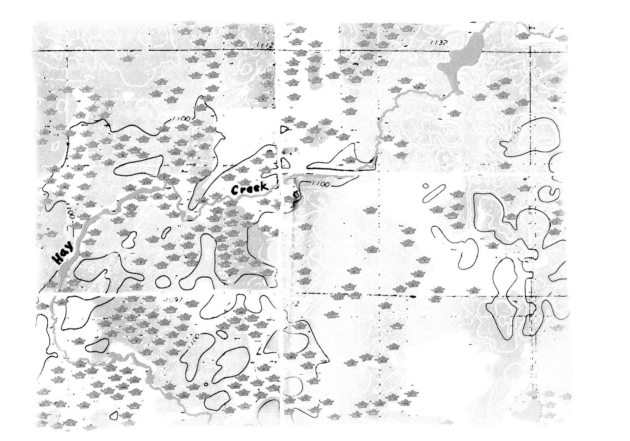

forested areas, and blue wetland hummocks), and if he continued to travel the same direction he was going, he couldn't miss Hay Creek along which the map shows broad expanses of hummocky wetlands, a blue stream and even some blue ponds. All of that was only one-and-a-quarter miles ahead. And once he found the stream, which he should have reached that same day, he'd have good going (for a muskrat) via Hay Creek into the Willow River, then on down the Kettle River, the St. Croix, and Mississippi, all the way to the Gulf of Mexico, if he so chose.

I think he's down on Hay Creek, sexually satisfied and cozy in a small shelter he built, with underwater entrances and a good supply of cattail roots and stems and other goodies nearby. And maybe he's built another feeding station where he can get to those fine sedge stems and have good places to sun on warm days.

One Week Later

I don't expect the muskrat back, but I did go down to check on his feeding station a week after he left. Several very light snows had covered all tracks. Some creature had rearranged the door plugs (probably he or she came up from below the ice). They were now frozen where they were left by the visitor. I pried three of the blobs loose to take home and analyze. Under one I found five bright red berries. They had kept their color like frozen foods from a supermarket, shining like cranberries, looking fresh picked.

On a hunch, I removed a mitten and held the berries in my bare hand. They quickly melted into one little puddle of blood.

The visitor, very likely a mink, must have come looking for lunch, and found a vole or a mouse in a little cave in the muskrat's feeding station.

Life goes on.

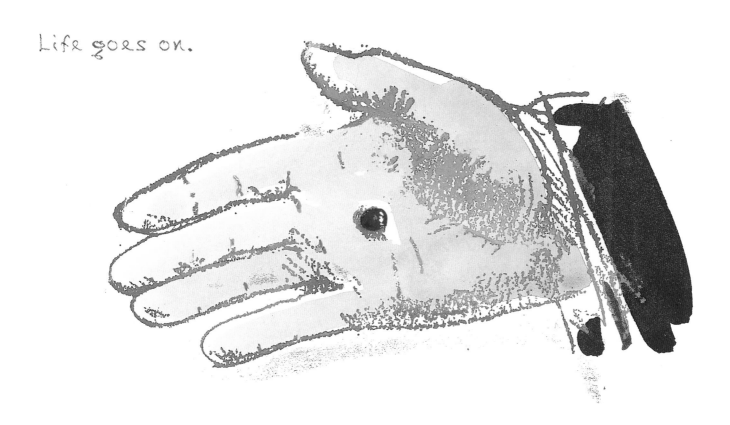

Blacklock Nature Sanctuary

Much of this story takes place on the Blacklock Nature Sanctuary. Each year artists, writers, choreographers and composers are provided residencies at the Sanctuary. They have access to the hundreds of acres of land preserved by the Sanctuary near Moose Lake, Minnesota, and on the North Shore of Lake Superior.

Originally a dream of the Blacklock family, the Sanctuary is now a well-established, non-profit organization with a unique mission: to protect, provide access to and advocate respect for significant natural environments. Through its programs and practices and following the examples set by the Blacklock family, the Sanctuary fosters creative growth through experience, study and interpretation of nature.

All proceeds from this book are being donated to the Sanctuary. To learn more about the Blacklock Nature Sanctuary please visit the web site: www.blacklock.org.

A special thank you to our friend David Garon at Digital Ink for converting Les' printing into the font used in this book.

Published by:
Blacklock Nature Photography
P.O. Box 570
Moose Lake MN 55767
218-485-8335

Distributed by:
Adventure Publications, Inc.
820 Cleveland Street South
Cambridge MN 55008
1-800-678-7006 &
1-877-725-0088

Printed in the Republic of Korea by Doosan Printing.
10 9 8 7 6 5 4 3 2 1
06 05 04 03 02   FIRST EDITION
ISBN 1-892472-12-0